T0137585

Broken Promises; Mended Lies

Inside the Mind of Tonea Melvin

Tonea Melvin

Order this book online at www.trafford.com
or email orders@trafford.com

Most Trafford titles are also available at major online book retailers.

Printed in the United States of America.

ISBN: 978-1-4269-5676-8 (sc)
ISBN: 978-1-4269-5776-5 (e)

Trafford rev. 02/17/2011

 www.trafford.com

North America & international
toll-free: 1 888 232 4444 (USA & Canada)
phone: 250 383 6864 ♦ fax: 812 355 4082

Table of Contents

Introduction: Why?

My name is Tonea. You can call me Nea, or Toni. I respond to anything, really. I am 15 years old, going on 16 in July and I am a sophomore in high school. I just got home from a whole day of holding back tears in most of my classes. Not just because math and history is that bad, but because...well, I actually don't know. Sometimes I just wake up with these moods, and I just don't want to be here at all. Guess it is just a typical part of this 'depression' thing my doctor keeps telling me about. I guess that's where my writing comes from as well. The only time I sit here and write in my journal is when I'm trying to figure things out or when I just need to get anything I have inside out. So, that brings me to, why? Why am I taking the time out to sit here and write to you? I have a story inside and I finally want to get it out, if you are interested. I use these poems and stories to express every thought that is inside of my mind. Normally, I don't like telling people about what goes on inside of me; I have a habit of wearing a mask all of the time. So, please excuse any confusion, cliques, or strangeness...I tried to get as much of my personality into the story as I could.

Where Do We Go From Here?

Trust Is...

Trust is a delicate and very vital part of any relationship. It is easily lost, so hard to gain, and hard to keep sometimes. There are so many songs, TV shows, and books that touch on this concept of trust. Trust is common, but the most important type of trust is the trust between you and your parents and vice-versa. Of course, I have had a lot of problems with this. There were so many times where I had to prove to my parents that they could trust me to do things; it comes with being a teenager. Lately, I've been seeing more of a problem with me not being able to fully trust my parents. Not being able to trust the people you should be able to trust the most hurts a lot. Once trust has been tampered with, it's ridiculously difficult to patch up the hole in the bond between anyone. For me, it is still tough and I can't seem to figure out how to take the time to realize how much is being sacrificed. Trust can really either screw everything up for you, or benefit you. Sometimes I wonder what will happen if this perception of trust wasn't honored as much as it should be.

Cycle of Broken Promises and Mended Lies

You are constantly trying to forget the pain and the feeling of loneliness he left you with when he claimed he wasn't thinking.

But all you can really think of is how hard it was to see everything you ever learned and knew about your bond together just slip away.

And how much harder it is when you are reminded every day of those perfect summer days that clearly will never be the same.

All you can feel is the constant ripping and tearing inside your soul; indescribable, throbbing pain you've never felt before.

The only way to illustrate what he cannot see is to tell him about the ongoing shots of love and hate that go through your body like bullets every day.

He breaks all of the promises but mends all of his lies, and leaves your wounds open and badly infected with this everlasting, foreign disease that he likes to call "Affection".

You do everything in your willing power to avoid the disastrous waves of emotion and high tides of confusion.

In the end, you realize you are failing to recall the vital information you need to keep on living.

You are a part of him, and he a part of you, so your only choice of surviving in this world and to avoid the chaos is to break the promises and mend the lies,

Causing you to spread this disease you both like to call "Affection".

Trust

I thought that I could trust you, but now I see that is over.

I came to you with open arms each day,

hoping that you were going to be the one to embrace my devotion;

that special person who was going to heal my everlasting pain.

I let you into my life, thinking that I wouldn't be hurt by your love and

your protection.

Then you refused to open your arms and love me back, the way that I

loved you.

I wanted you to be the one; the one that was going to be by my side,

to make sure that I wasn't going to rely on the razor to love me the

way I thought no one else should.

But now my thoughts have changed, and my life has changed again.

I am back to my old ways and my old habits;

relying on that razor to be the only love I will receive.

I thought that I could trust you but you brought my life right back

down.

So now I'm letting you go and I'm finally going to say my last goodbye.

Don't say I love you and don't say you won't live without me

because those days have gone and I have already moved on.

Moment of Truth

She was sitting in her room alone on a Friday night, blasting music from her iHome, and speaking to her friends from New York on Facebook. Not many people are in the dorm tonight, everyone went out to have fun, and excluded her. Half of her feels fine; no worries and all fun and laughs online. The other half know something is about to happen. She silently agrees to listen to the half of her that is anticipating the worst. Then, she is startled by the loud music of Paramore, telling her that she has a phone call. It's her father. She can't fathom why he would be calling her; he hasn't spoken to her since Wednesday, besides the 5 minute talk they had earlier today. The typical conversation starts, but something is different. The tone of his voice is different. It seems worried and hesitated; not like the normal calm and confident voice she always hears. Here's where everything goes downhill.

Father: We've been lying to each other.

Girl: What?

Father: I haven't been totally honest with you; you haven't been honest with me.

Girl's thoughts: *Well duh! Want to explain more, father?*

Girl: Um, I'm confused. What are you talking about?

Father: Why did you ask me about my phone earlier?

Girl: Well, Aunty texted me randomly, and told me that your phone was messed up or something, and you couldn't call me or text me. Then I asked mom what happened, and she said you lost the phone, so she cut it off so nothing will happen to it. Then, I wanted to know what you were going to say, so I asked you and you said something else. Three stories just don't make sense to me.

Father: You thought I wouldn't tell you the truth?

Girl: ...Well, umm, err, well...no...but...uh

Father: Well you were right. Like I said, we both haven't been very honest lately. What really happened to my phone was...

Girl's thoughts: WELL? Don't just stand there, spit it out! What happened with you and mother now? What more crap could you guys possibly pull me into, huh?

She hangs up the phone, terrified of what her father just told her. There are tears streaming down her face and emotions bursting inside of her. She gathers just enough strength to confirm what just happened with her mother, only to be torn down again to a totally different story. Who does she believe? She feels her mother sounds more rational, more truthful. Then again, she feels that what her father told her an hour ago might be true as well. He would never give her false information.

She cries in her bed the rest of the night. She is alone, scared, confused, and worried. She is trying to answer questions and fill in details that have been left out. Why has her family decided to tear her apart and betray the last pieces of trust they had between each other? Why did God allow things to get this far, and why is he making everything so hard? Will she find no light at the end of the tunnel? Is there no miracle to pull her through or a hero that can fly in and save her?

There is only she, and her broken bits of false truth, her family, and her heart scattered on the floor falling deeper and deeper into oblivion.

Love

What's Love Got to Do With It?

What is love? I have no idea, and I'm not really going to try to define it, because it's a complicated subject. Most of the time, teens think love will always be there. We always manage to find this magnetic connection within each one of our boyfriends and girlfriends, whether it really be true or not. There is always something about somebody that we like a lot, and we jump right to the 'L' word. I think that is a total waste of time. Tina Turner was absolutely right to question love and its intensity. Who can really pin-point what love is, and why it is significant for anything. Of course, love is a charming idea, and everyone would like to experience what it feels like at least once in their life, but once it is over what are you going to do? Personally, I try to stay away from the misleading word whenever I can. I have used it a couple of times, but then I realized that it was a total mistake. You see, in my world, love is just an excuse and as my father always used to tell me, excuses are nothing but admissions into failure. I know this sounds harsh, but after Seeing how miserable my parents were when they were "in love", and how it didn't help them at all when the love was gone, I think it is very appropriate to discard of this profound 4-letter word until you feel like it is absolutely necessary to use it. When you do think it is necessary, keep in mind that it might go away, maybe not soon, but eventually, it might. Come to think about it, I don't believe in anything that has to do with love. I try to enjoy the corny, clique romantic comedies all of my friends watch, but it is extremely hard when all I can think of is how fake it all is or what would have happened if they extended the movie. It would be nearly impossible for those two characters to survive in a relationship after those couple of months. Of course I love my family and friends, but that is totally different from what I am trying to explain. The only love that really should be recognized is love of self. Without loving yourself, it is really impossible to love anyone else. It's ironic that I'm writing a whole section dedicated to Love, right?

Until I see you again

I'm sitting here in English, trying to concentrate on the translated words of Sophocles, but all I can really think about is your charismatic smile.

It's a typical rainy, winter Wednesday and I'm daydreaming and wishing once more to see you again.

Every now and again, I sneak a little pinch and hope that being away from you is just another one of my unimaginable thoughts.

These days drag on while slowly getting longer and I still can't figure out when I can see you again.

I'm counting down the hours; Imagining and feeling your gentle touch. I can still catch the chills that pass through me when you wrap your arms around me.

I can hear your voice whispering your angelic words into my ears, charming me with each kiss between.

Tick tock goes the clock…

30…29…28…there goes the days running out the door;

All of these thoughts run through my mind;

as I comfort myself and say "This month won't be too long;

We will soon see each other again".

Letter to Love

Dear Love (or whatever your name is):

All I want to say is thank you. First and foremost, thank you for your help. Every day I sat by the window, looking out at the year's snow in the winter, its colors in the fall, its flowers in the spring, and the millions of kids running around in the summer. I would let life pass me by thinking you were too busy helping my friends to even say hello to me. Then you finally became one of my best friends and you introduced me to my first love. Thank you for those 4 months of happiness with the person you said was going to be "the one". I spent those days thinking about him every minute. Visualizing and anticipating his touch and his warm, surprising kisses. It was the first time I felt like I belonged. I was no longer the third wheel, or the "other friend" with no one to spend her evenings with. You convinced me that he was my everything; that every breath, every step, and every thought was all for him, when in reality, he didn't even care at all.

Thank you for letting me down and showing me how horrible love can be when it ends. You showed me how to cry for someone. I learned how to look at everyone else as they were just going to betray me, just like you and he did. By leaving me in the dark, you even helped me discover parts of myself I never knew existed; like I was in a totally different world. A world where all I listened to was alternative and Indie rock music, wrote depressing poems about lies and deceit, and got to know new people who were just like me.

Thanks again for everything. I really enjoyed being your prisoner and letting you make a fool out of me. We really had some good times together, but this time, it is me who is going to run away from you. You are going to be the one to feel ignored and alone. Don't even bother to worry about me, because I will be just fine sitting here listening to Paramore and telling the world about how much betrayal hurts. Goodbye. I really hope I won't see you again.

Thanks,
~~Tonea~~ Your Anonymous Victim

The Thought that Counts

What Goes On Up There?

Do you ever just sit there in your bed, staring at the ceiling, just Wondering what's really happing in your mind? Ever take the time to think about the things you usually think about? Maybe it's just me being weird and over-analytical like always. Sometimes I catch myself trying to figure out the random tangents that go on inside my mind. After reading *Girl, Interrupted* by Susana Kaysen, I often catch myself thinking more about everything. A lot of the times, I'm trying to figure the mess in my mind. The thoughts in my head are best decried as utter confusion. I'm forever thinking of a million things at once, none of which relating to the other. I find myself lost in my mind, as well. I take chances and travel roads that lead me to other unfinished thoughts. I never know if I should try to finish them. The freaky thing is, my deepest and most intense thoughts show up in the dreams. Those are the worst times. I always carry thoughts from my dreams with me throughout the day. I get so into my dreams and previous thoughts that they turn into daydreams in class and most of the time they turn into poems and stories. It's all so abstract and weird, but I can't seem to ever find a way to tell myself to stop exploring. I guess I just haven't found that thought yet. I'll have to make a note to find it later...

Morning Nightmares

Its 3:45 AM and I've been awaken again by my past. My eyes are wide open, my mind alert and I'm focused on the reoccurring question that is fresh in my mind. Trying to block everything out to get my last 3 hours of sleep, I close my eyes again and pray that these recollections that happen every morning won't disturb me again today. First, everything hits me, and it feels like a boulder of emotions coming at me instantaneously. Then, I start to ask myself, "Why am I still alive; why has He let me survive another dreaded night?" I can't seem to understand why I am here, in this suffering position. While I'm still half-asleep and trying to answer these questions, horrible flashbacks of last night's nightmares begin to haunt me. I step into the shower hoping that the trickles of water coming out of the cold, metallic spout will wash away the dreaded nightmares of the night before. The images of the crimson red river rolling down my arms and wrists return over and over. As I fight to remove these images out of my head, I shiver once again failing to let go of my intense past. The only thing I am left to do to try to let go is to pack all of the emotions and flashbacks up with me, as I throw my books in my bag and proceed to walk down the white winter road that leads me to the classroom building for another day of unforgotten pain.

Confusion

Your mind is emptied out of all concern and you know you have to do it.

You begin, and then all of a sudden, you start to ask a million questions.

Where am I? How did I get here? What did I do to deserve this?

Who is going to be there to help me?

Where is everyone going? Why do I feel so alone?

Questions everywhere; Emotions flowing all over your mind and you can't figure out how this scene is going to end.

The confusion starts to overflow and your head feels like it is going to burst into a thousand pieces.

Can you keep up with this chaos that's going on up there?

How are you going to stop it? Will it ever stop?

You come to your final thoughts.

No more time for asking questions, just do what you came to do, even though you can't remember what that is.

You can't stop now but the pressure is way too much to handle.

You see the blood on your hands, but you can't remember why it's there.

Then the chaos dies down, no more questions and no more answers as you blankly stare at the ceiling.

No more confusion.

Reality VS Fantasy:
My Toughest Times

What Can I Say?

I don't have much to say about the tough times I had and still have to go through. It all speaks for itself, really. When you are going through tough times, whether it is extremely hard or simple, it's going to take a toll on your life for the moment, and a lot of times you feel lonely, and you don't know where to go. I feel like this almost every day, and I'm pretty sure it's normal. Living at a boarding school, not being able to see my mother, not being able to help my parents when they need it, and not being able to do the things I am used to at home all make it hard to be in another state away from my family. The hardest part about everything is having to bring back some of the good memories in order to remind myself of the things that are eventually going to work out. Sometimes the memories don't work; they just make things worse. I try to think of the late nights on the porch I would spend talking with my father about sports and the crazy stories about the family or, the late Sunday mornings I would spend with my mother watching complicated television shows, but all it ever does is make me yearn for those days and nights even more. Telling people that I will be okay, and I will get over the homesickness is definitely easier said than done. It does help to be distracted by the loads of work, but once that is all done, what am I supposed to do with the extra two hours before I fall asleep. All I can do is count down the days until I can go back home and do all that I can to fill in for the weeks that I have missed. Making up for lost time is the worst, especially when you have to make up a whole month of occurrences that was lost, all in a couple of days. Tough times are... tough. It takes a while to get through them, but it happens eventually. I'm still going through a lot, but I'm glad that I finally have people who are trying to help me through the best that they can.

Her Call for Help

Every night she screamed, "Someone save me!"

But no one ever listened.

Every day her eyes shed tears,

But no one ever saw.

Every evening she was reminded of the night before

When she took that sharp edge, made those incisions

And let the pain run out with blood.

But no one bothered to question her acts.

From the brightness of the dawn,

Until the darkness of the midnight's sky,

She thought, *why me? Why am I the only one feeling this way?*

But no one ever answered.

Then one night, she decided she wasn't going to cry herself to sleep,

And she was going to try to deal with the pain on her own.

She went to sleep, but she never woke up.

Now everyone tries to ask:

What happened? Why? And then they realize,

They should have paid attention to her call for help.

Just Too Good To Stay the Same

A major part of my life right now revolves around change. Everything that happens now is totally different from how things used to be. Some of the big changes are happening to my family, my feelings, and even my memories. I am still learning how to get used to these changes. I'm getting much better, but some things are so much harder to contain than others. What makes it harder to take in is I really don't know why all of these changes are taking place. All I know is the general stuff. Mom and dad don't love each other anymore, so dad moves out, we have to figure out custody arrangements, and then my life is just supposed to go on. My question is why? Why do I have to go through all of this and why does any of this even exist? I think I should have, at least been warned that not everything will stay the same. Or that mommy and daddy might not always be together, like I always thought they would. I was happy to be one out of five kids in a 15-student grade that was actually able to say that I had two happily married parents who were always there for me. It never occurred to me that I could be like the other ten kids who had broken families and a parent that couldn't/ wasn't always there to catch them when they fell. I never pictured hearing different footsteps walking up the stairs and into my mother's room. I never knew that I could be one of those kids who say that they have a stepdad. All of the changes in my life came so fast, I didn't even notice they were happening until things started to settle down. I'm still trying to figure out how feelings can change so drastically, too. One day you can be completely care-free, loving, full of hope and pride; the next day all you feel is despair, pain and hatred. I don't understand how all of those feelings managed to live together in my heart and soul. I feel them fighting sometimes though. When the acing inside gets stronger and stronger with each beat, that's when they are fighting the most. I guess it's going to take a lot of time and patience to get used to this new life full of changes all over. Wish me luck.

Unanswered Questions

Questions that I can't seem to answer scare me. Not the questions that I get asked in school about World War II or a character in *Jane Eyre*, questions about life and questions people ask me about myself. Even simple questions like "What do you want to do after college?" I always manage to stress myself out about why I don't know and what is going to happen to me if I never figure it out. Most of the time after I'm done stressing out about it, I can move on and just accept that it will take time before I can truthfully answer those questions, except for the time my mother asked me the most terrifying question I had ever been asked.

One day, after getting into serious trouble the night before, I woke up and there was a message on my desk from my mother. Essentially, my mother had asked me "Who is Tonea?" This was the worst, most difficult question anyone could have ever asked me. The part that scared me the most, of course, was I couldn't even think of the simplest answer to give her. It frightened me so much that I couldn't figure out exactly who I was. I cried and cried, trying to think of ways to answer. I practically racked my brain and I couldn't think of anything at all. After an hour of sitting on my bed and staring up at my ceiling, I decided to just write something. I told my mother that I had no idea who Tonea is. I told her that sometimes Tonea is a perfectly happy, normal child that enjoys life and what is being offered to her. There isn't a problem in the world that can bring her down, especially when she is certain that her family is totally fine. On the other hand, there are a lot of days where Tonea is one of those lost children in the dark who thinks of nothing but suicide and constantly asks herself why she is even alive. By the end of the whole part where I had to explain to my mother that I had no idea who Tonea is, I wrote a little note at the end, telling her that I was going somewhere. I went to my godmother's house for the night, which was probably the best idea I had in a while. I couldn't be smothered by the intensity of my fears anymore. I needed time to calm down and realize that it was actually okay not knowing exactly who I was. My godmother helped me recognize that discovering yourself, knowing who you are, and who you want to become, are all parts of growing up. I'm so glad that happy endings really exist.

About the Author

Tonea Melvin is a 15 year old, educated Dana Hall student who has a passion for writing. Melvin uses her poems and stories to express herself in ways that she normally wouldn't. Her poems are mostly related to her feeling and things she experiences everyday in her life. Tonea Melvin currently is a boarding student at the Dana Hall School, in Wellesley, Massachusetts, but often goes back to her home town in Bronx, New York.